The boat and the tower

The stories of Noah and the Tower of Babel

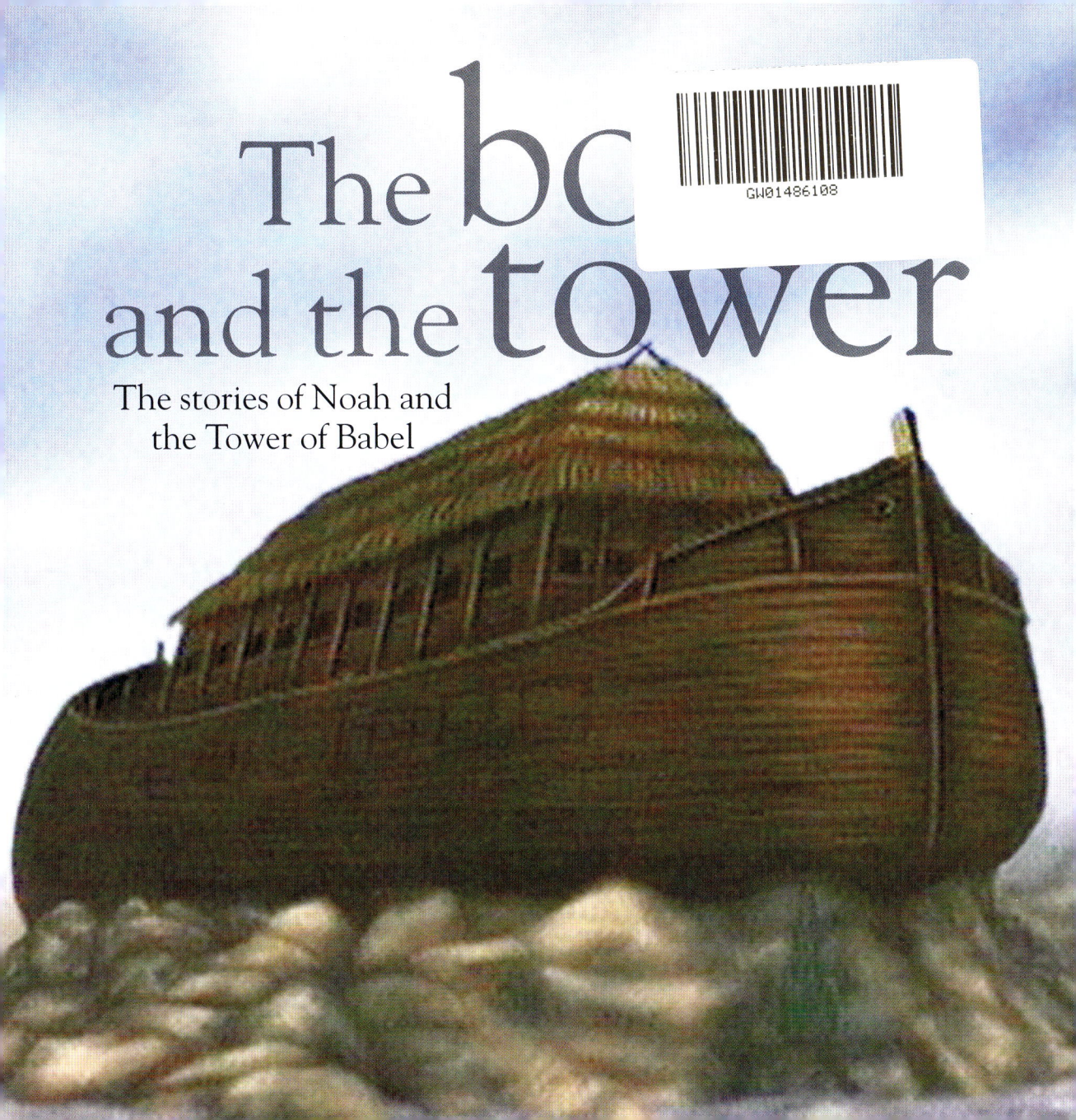

The Story so Far

JON couldn't get on with his homework. He had to write about a love story, and it had to come from the Bible. 'Love stories are for wimps,' he moaned.

His computer mouse whisked him through the computer screen, through space and time into a book-filled study. There he met the Scribe.

'I'll show you a love story,' said the Scribe.

The Scribe took Jon back to the time when God made Adam and Eve and a fabulous Garden. An evil angel called Satan persuaded Adam and Eve to rebel against God. They were thrown out, but the damage was done. A virus had come into the Earth.

God still loved his people and with his help, Eve had two sons, Cain and Abel. But Cain was treacherous. Seething with jealousy, he murdered Abel. The virus was at work.

"Hey! It's raining. It's teeming down. I'm getting soaked. Where've you brought me?"

 "We were in the middle of a love story, remember. I wish I'd brought my brolly! It's a bit slippy! Oh – ah – ahhhh!"

"Where's my mouse?
Gotcha, little mouse."

The Scribe hauled himself out of the water.

"That's right, rescue your mouse!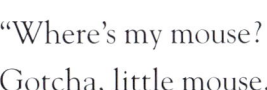
Don't bother about me."

 "What's happened?
There's nothing but water everywhere."

"Remember what I told you?
Shema!"

 "I've not forgotten! It means 'listen'. But where are we?"

3

"Where are we? We're where we were when we left Cain. But hundreds of years later. His children had children and they had children and on and on. They built villages and cities. But the people were bad. They were murderous. And devilish. Scum.

"God was sad when he looked at his world. His heart was filled with pain."

"Was everyone like that?"

"There was one man who loved God."

"That one good man was Noah. God said to Noah, 'I'm sorry I made the people on the Earth. I intend to destroy them. But I'll keep you and your family safe. This is my plan. You must build a boat.'"

"Wasn't it cruel to kill all the people?"

"The people were cruel to one another. They were vicious.

"When Noah started building, they called him all the names you can imagine – and more. "Nutty Noah!" they yelled. "You're bonkers! Where's the sea?'

"Noah warned them. 'It's not 'too late," he said. 'Tell God you're sorry. He'll give you another chance.'

""Noah's flipped,' they said."

 "What did Noah do?"

"He got on with the boat. And his sons helped him. Ham, Shem and Japheth their names were. Their wives helped, too. It was a family project, you might say."

 "God gave Noah the exact plans for the ark. It was massive, longer than a football field and taller than the Statue of Liberty. It had one door, three decks, and small windows all the way round, just under the roof. Inside there were hundreds of little rooms."

 "Were those for the animals?"

"Yes, and for the birds, and reptiles and insects. God told Noah to get one pair of every kind of 'unclean' creature, that means, creatures that couldn't be eaten, and seven pairs of every kind of 'clean' creature, the sort that could be eaten."

 "What about food and water?"

"Noah collected hundreds of bags and baskets of fruit and vegetables and nuts. But not water. Water was one thing they weren't going to need.

"Noah did everything God told him to do. It took years. But the day came when everything was ready."

"God said, 'It's time. Go on board.' So they did. And God shut the door.

"For seven days nothing happened. Then a wind blew up. Clouds drifted across the sky. They hid the sun. A few drops of rain began to fall."

"What did the people do?"

"No one was laughing now.

"The rain fell harder. The clouds poured down water. And underground rivers and fountains surged up."

"It was the flood."

 "For forty days the rain fell, pelting down on the roof of the ark. Then suddenly, everything went quiet. The rain had stopped."

 "Hurrah!"

"Eeeeek!"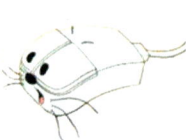

 "But that wasn't the end. For another 110 days the water kept on rising. It covered the highest mountains."

"Where are we? It's so gloomy, I can hardly see. What a stink! What a row!"

"What do you expect, with all these animals and birds? We're inside the ark, of course. And I must say, it is a bit stuffy. But the roof is fastened down. No one can get out.

"They've all been shut up in here for 224 days – that's about eight months."

"Isn't the food running out? Aren't they scared that this floating zoo will turn into a floating coffin?"

"Noah's not scared. He knows God loves them. Anyway, the water's now going down."

"Hey – what's that scraping, creaking noise. Hey! Oooo-er, I'm falling! The boat's rocking. Mr Scribe, what's happening?"

"The boat's come to ground, to be more accurate, to mountain top. It's stuck on Mount Ararat, in the land you call Turkey."

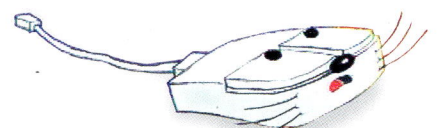

"Great, we can all get out!"

"People aren't eagles. They can't live on mountains. Have the floods gone on the low lands?"

"Can't Noah look out of the window?"

"He can only see sky from those high windows. Noah sends out a raven. It doesn't come back. So he sends out a homing pigeon. All day it swoops over the water – and returns in the evening. He waits a

week and sends it out again. It comes back carrying an olive leaf."

"Everyone's cheering."

"That's because olive trees grow in the foothills. The flood's over. But Noah wants to be sure. He waits a week, and sends out the bird again. It doesn't come back."

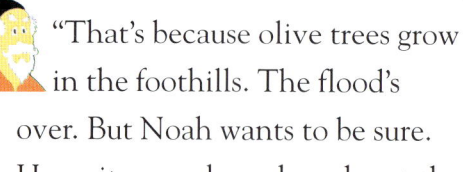

 "Noah takes off the covering from the top of the ark. They all look out and see thick squelchy mud! Glorious mud! But they can't get out. It's too wet."

"How long do we have to wait?"

 "Time for a party!"

"First it's time to thank God. Noah calls his family together and they pray to God. And God has a message for Noah."

"After eight more weeks, God says, 'Bring everyone out of the ark.' So they all come out – jumping and leaping, and slithering and hopping and skipping and twirling and flying. And Noah says, 'Go free! Make a new world.'"

"Look! There's a rainbow!"

"That's God's sign. God says, 'I'm making a covenant with you.'"

"What's a covenant?"

"It's a pact, an agreement. God promises that he'll never again kill all the life on Planet Earth. As long as the Earth lasts there will be summer and winter, seedtime and harvest. The rainbow is to remind people – it's like an engagement ring.

"And God says, 'Now be happy, all of you.'

"But right from the start of their new life things began to go wrong."

"What are all those people doing?"

"Hundreds of years have gone by since the time of Noah. The people have planted their crops, and rebuilt their villages and towns and cities. They think they're so wonderful.

"'Let's make a name for ourselves!' they say. 'Let's build a tower that touches the sky. We'll be famous for ever.'

"They set about making loads of bricks."

"My dad always says, 'Pride goes before a fall.'"

"They're not planning on falling. They're calling their tower 'Babel', which means, 'Gateway to a god'. But they don't stop to ask God what he thinks."

"All those power-mad people are saying, 'Come on! If we stick together, we'll be invincible. We'll be able to do anything.'

"That's dangerous talk."

"So what does God do? Does he send a bolt of lightning from the sky?"

"No need. He muddles up their language into different languages. They get very cross indeed. 'Talk sense, can't you?' they yell.

"The tower never gets finished. They split up and go off to live in different places. They're famous all right: famous for failing."

"So was that the end of the love story?'"

"No – God never stopped loving his people.

"Do you remember that virus that came into the world when Adam and Eve turned against God? It twisted people so that they didn't want to love him.

"But there was always at least one person who loved God."

 "Like Noah?"

"Yes, and God saved Noah and his family. Well, God has a long-term  strategy. He's going to save his world. He plans to begin with one man. But that's a new chapter in God's love story."

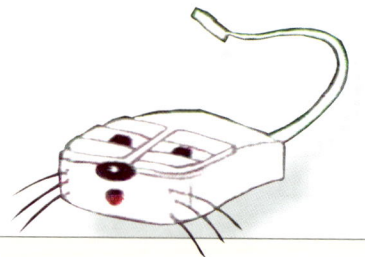

These stories are in the Bible. You can find the story of Noah and the ark in Genesis chapters 6–9, and the story of the Tower of Babel in Genesis chapter 11.